AF669548

A Poem Is

Don Kingfisher Campbell

Contents

ISBN: 978-81-19654-09-3 Cyberwit.net

Dedicated to my wife Aihua Gao

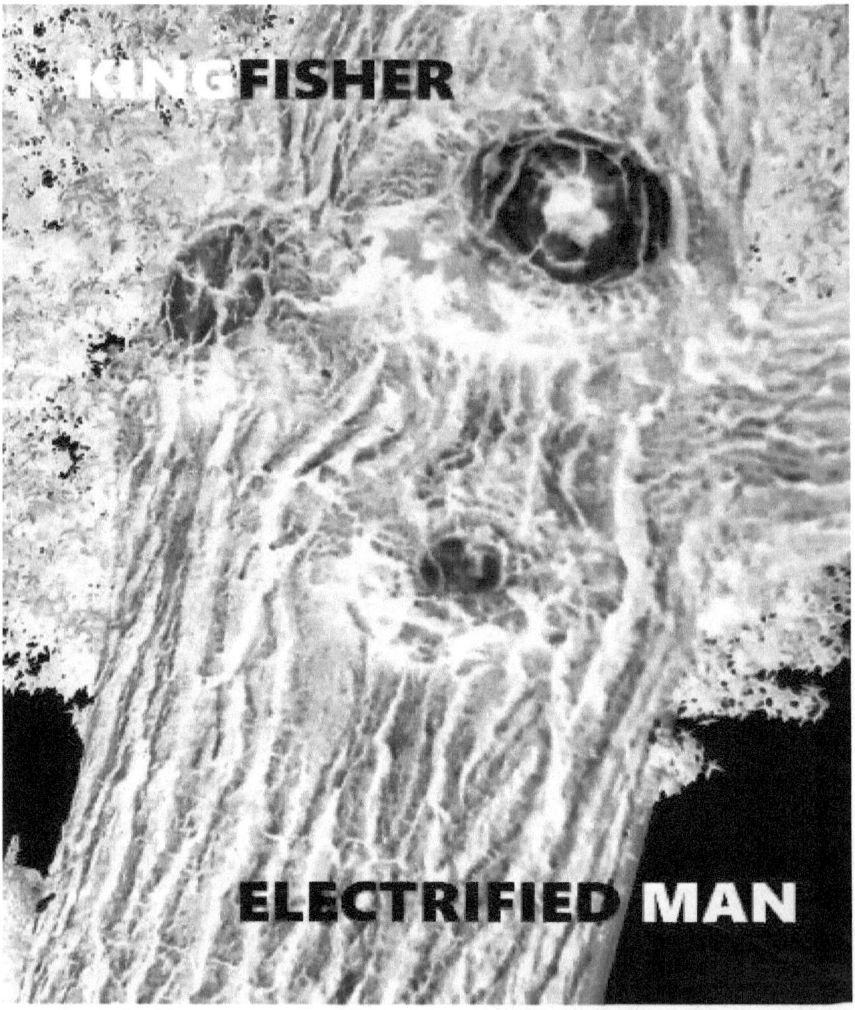

1 > Fall (06 04 2022)
2 > Snake and Pig (06 05 2022)
3 > Sukie Strikes Again! (06 20 2022)
4 > Details (06 30 2022)
5 > White Gloves (07 02 2022)
6 > Stellar Sonnet (07 12 2022)
7 > Fencing (07 23 2022)
8 > News (07 23 2022)
9 > Electrified man screams he can’t leave his little house (08 07 2022)
10 > She is a firework in my life (08 17 2022)
11 > Dew Drops on a Dead Leaf (08 25 2022)
12 > She’s Gone (09 03 2022)

1 > **Fall**

When the first white hairs
popped out of my beard,
I knew my summer was ending.

The 40's, my fifth decade,
had begun, and it was time
to embrace the dad bod.

Oldies stations started to play
80's pop. Students calling me
Santa Claus's younger brother.

Circumstances made me
single again as I turned 50.
What to do after so many years
of domestic complacency.

I looked to my friend
the internet for ideas. All
it offered me was more
porno and dating websites.

Finding a date was easier than
expected, but find someone you
want to marry, that's different.
There are qualifications.

Not too young, not too old,
not too tall, not too short,
not too fat, not too skinny,
not too brainy, not too stupid,
and that was me gazing in the
mirror at my own reflection.

Entering my seventh decennium,
beyond the trial and error of
my 50's, I finally met another
person with the same dream.

Now we can look forward
together to the proliferation
of age spots, blood and urine
test results, and the gradual
decline of our abilities.

At least our winter might
not be lonely, if we are faithful
to the future, we will be
rewarded with maybe two
possibly three tens of memories.

2 > **Snake and Pig**

She misses sitting at a round table
with her friends for the Dragon
Boat Festival watching delicious
dishes and drinks carousel around.

They send each other WeChat
photos and videos. Hers, of the
flora and fauna we encounter or
the legendary discount and outlet
stores I drive her to shop in.

On her cellphone she also listens
to music of her homeland, looks
at funny and informative TikTok
postings of biracial domestic
relationships and crafty cooking,
whiling away the hours I spend
reading, writing, publishing poetry
or absorbing YouTube songs
and controversial comedians.

Sometimes we sit on pushed together
oversized cushiony massage chairs
for a couple experience when we're
lucky enough to find a mutual interest,
like The Squid Game, NBA basketball,
or The Hospital, a Taiwan soap opera
featuring world famous Asian stars.

She was a nurse for 22 years in
the communist China navy. Still
gets a meager pension, rents out
rooms in her island and mainland
"houses", really multi-story condos.

Yet here she is seeking lifelong love
and security, a home in America,
specifically California, because her new
husband is a native, raised in Monterey
Park, so my taste in women made us a
match formed in handheld internet
haven.

And trust Google translates every day
conversations, so we can communicate
like a regular pair of loving humans,
trying to comfort one another in a
world troubled by superficialities
like race, gender, religion, and politics.

In our own duplex existence we
happily execute meals, shopping
trips, even sex, as if we were grown
schoolchildren becoming old
partners, playfully sharing our
discoveries, revelations, and feelings.

We have learned to confide in being
mated beings, the breathing lifeforms,
chemically bonded through eyes,
arms, lips, and fluid exchange.

3 > **Sukie Strikes Again!**

She's back but she's missing
a left eye completely
wearing a clear plastic
cone to prevent clawing
of the sewn-up furry socket

Sukie walks just the same
now with cylindrical scrapes
bumping into chairs and tables
Mina straps her into her harness
leads her out the front door
to pace down the empty driveway
turn onto the comforting sidewalk

Sukie hates lawn edges
steers away when she touches
one like it's a video game
she especially disdains
stepping on fallen seed pods
doesn't like the hard crunch
under her soft black paw pads

She does her usual sudden turns
into the street, blindly startled
stepping off curbs, almost
walking straight into cars
only to be discreetly redirected
with Mina's gentle guidance

Sukie eventually senses
a patch of dirt and clump
growth just right to pee on
a long trail runs onto concrete
as it would for any human

After many walks for three days
Sukie finally poo-pooed
this morning like a senior
squeezing out mushy cigars

So, success! Mina is happy
she did it, we triumphantly
return to our home and Mina
the retired nurse dutifully cleans
her butt thoroughly using alcohol
wipes her daughter provided

Then we get a text message
they are coming tomorrow
to reclaim their beloved
rescue, aw, such a short
weekend Sukie chapter
for us and the twelve year old
dogecoin doppelganger

4 > **Details**

a high
chain-link
fenced city
playground

news crews
scattered
around
the sidewalk

prepare
to camera
transmit and
microphone
cover

but will it be
what I notice

a pink
teddy bear
tied to
a tree
by stretched
white police
tape that
says in
blue letters
DO NOT CROSS

pink roses
lie at
the bottom
of the tree

a big
long
darkened
blood
stain

on the gray
pebbly sidewalk
next to

a BRUTE
brand gray
plastic trash
handled barrel

with a dozen
pink roses
wrapped in
cellophane
leaning
against it

parked
at the curb
a Smart car

doors labeled
"roadway moving"
has two white
silhouetted stick
people carrying
a blue heart
on the hood

on a nearby
tree support
a torn remnant
of police tape
is now only
CROSS

someone
gave out
a pink
candlelight
vigil flyer

from WE ALL
REALLY MATTER
Domestic
Violence
Organization

in memory of
Azsia Johnson

5 > **White Gloves**

a single glove lies on
the shelf, inspiration,

a souvenir of the Wednesday
funeral I was a pall bearer for

a fortmorning ago four of us
carried the casket out of the

hearse onto the collapsible
waiting bier wheeled over

to the steps where we had to
lift again to the church entrance

once more to be rested on the
conveyor, walked down the aisle

maintaining one gloved hand
on the long smooth rod handle

to the front of the sanctuary
took our seats for the service

words were said and echoed
I hadn't been here since 1985

everything looked the same 37
years after my father's ceremony

I only remembered just then
they had donated the expense

of the carved fourteenth station
plaque still hanging on the wall

going in to six decades, it felt
familiar to be back amongst

the polished wood pews and
the swinging smoking censer

when prayers were finished
we resumed our positions

paced the oblong container
toward double double doors

to return the encased body
to the black station wagon

for the ride to the cemetery
and the final carrying over

other headstoned mounds
to lay down one last time

the sarcophagus that held
what was left of my mother

an autopsied shell hidden
in a closed rectangular box

it had the weight of a woman
soon to be lowered to rest

on top of her husband as was
arranged ages before we sat

all these episodes later, people
saying thoughts out loud

though I was silent, masked,
my brain filled with memories

of a childhood spent with parents
and my escape to my own traumas

and triumphs chronicled in poems
of which this one restrains refrains

from saying too much out of
respect for a life tangent to mine

now I am the eldest member
of my acknowledged family

I must continue to try to set an
example for my adult children

on how to let go of the passed
in rows gently recalling the wake

6 > **Stellar Sonnet**

These photographs
of what
we once were

Show that color
existed before
we had eyes

That clouds
of dust dance
into orbits ignite

Around each other
attracted coming
closer colliding

Joining to form
stars planets
moons asteroids

Consisting of
gas some
cooling solid

Cells activating
swirling wriggle
to combine

And become
little beings
in water

Then sand and dirt
and plant allowed
further evolution

To upright animals
creating telescopes
to hope to see

Their own
birthplace again
this time

Knowing from those
cosmic cliffs
we walk today

And will return
to renew the great
cycles of eons

(Doesn't that
nebula look like
a stuffed teddy bear)

7 > **Fencing**

A long time ago I used to
lean on a fence to watch
my son play on a playground

That's just a memory

I've seen fences used to keep people
from stepping on plants, pilfering trees

Those got old too

Now my new wife daydreams
about our future house and
its fenced herbs and vegetables

My mind likes to wrap
itself around that idea

8 > **News**

I could go off making donuts
on the just opened 6th St bridge

I could disappear amidst a crowd
and emerge with a new strain

I could produce a gun in my car
and get shot and killed by police

I could fly a plane into the ocean
and be rescued by beachgoers

(during the 2022 California Surf Lifesaving
Association Junior Lifeguard Championship, no less)

I could pay the rent or buy
a single Springsteen ticket

I could put my money through a machine and hope
a string of numbers will come my way (maybe)

No, I think I'll do the miracles I do
every day I wake up and hug my wife

9 > **Electrified man screams he can't leave his little house**

My brain is surrounded by a fence

My mind is a lion god worshipping a bed of roses

My soul is a cat sitting on a windowsill watching leaves dance

My eyes have been wishing they could climb branches by themselves for decades

My mouth is a troubled door opening wide for a blast of stones

My belly is a flying saucer ready to fly high above the clouds

My penis is an aloe vera plant that transforms into a palm tree

My legs are afraid of becoming pudgy gnomes

My feet are beer cans tossed through the gate of the future

10 > **She is a firework in my life**

She makes my heart go boom

My breaths fall away like dominoes

My body wants to get on her bicycle

And ride, ride, ride until my mind

Until her mind says the train

Our train is coming to the station

And I hug security and comfort

We have become family I plan

We plan our day and then we act

Shower dress breakfast brush exit

Into the optimistic world that is ours

And I pray we'll have decades we

Knowing our forms age as we go

Forward into unforeseeable future

11 > **Dew drops on a dead leaf**

The giant goes for a walk
under the blazing sun

The behemoth steps and steps
on long concrete sidewalk

A small insect traverses the
width of a rectangle just ahead

One gargantuan sandal darkens
the sky above the bug only briefly

It was the last thing it ever felt,
a mindless accident of location

12 > **She's Gone**

Returned to her masters
All that is left are
Tufts on the rug
Hairs all over my car's back seat
An empty spot by the front door
Where her aluminum pie pan food dish
And black plastic water trough
Lay for a whole month
Us watching Sukie
Shift lying positions on the vinyl flooring
To sleep through the heat wave
Getting up to nudge me in my chair
That she had a need
To walk with her "grandmother"
(that I should fetch her)
And she harnesses the Shiba Inu up
Leads her outside to traverse
Sidewalks like it was pinball
For the blind doggie dog
Averse to scraping grass edges
Until a smell is smelt
Making her step across blades
To sniff inspiration to pee and poop
Circle around and squat
Squeeze to let out a stream
Even better soft cigars
I am handed the leash
So my wife can pick up clumps
With a paper napkin
All of us going back home
That she may flush
Then mealtime she stands near us
Soliciting morsels of meat
The daily cycle continuing
Wake walk discharge eat sleep
Each day structured for her schedule
And today it is hot again, the fan blows
Remnant strands of Sukie

1 > Impressions of September LV (09 08 2022)
2 > The Richest Homeless Guy in Vegas (09 16 2022)
3 > You and Me (10 01 2022)
4 > Tulare Trek (10 05 2022)
5 > Sequoia Sojourn (10 06 2022)
6 > Still Life (10 07 2022)
7 > The Gap (10 09 2022)
8 > Appreciation (11 05 2022)
9 > Some Things to Do on This Planet (11 20 2022)
10 > In the World War III Museum (11 23 2022)
11 > Things to Remember Before the War (11 23 2022)
12 > From the Blue Bible, Onward… (11 27 2022)

1 > **Impressions of September LV**

Shiny skyscraping hotels line the I-15

Casino themed car-filled boulevards

Tanned homeless slumping along sidewalks

110 degree heat thickens the cloudless air

Mattresses left curbside in front of too many houses

Cultural businesses just like any other city

Palm trees and pools seen outside tower room windows

Post-pandemic non-emptiness in smoky gambling halls

Man-made entertainment volcano blasts night fire

Balding retired men escort their women to $100 a ticket shows

Neighborhoods of stuccoed homes in named clusters

The whole desert valley ringed by highways

2 > **The Richest Homeless Guy in Vegas**

On a street
running parallel
to a freeway

On the corner
where the road
angles left

There is a triangular
space between house
and sound wall

There is a man
who stands outside
his old camper

He looks up
at the sun
long bearded

He feels kinda safe
behind his makeshift
wood board fence

I think to myself
here is someone
without a mortgage

I am a bit envious
of his simple life in a
world famous sin city

The only way for this
paradise to prematurely
end is official intervention

The day that happens
will be a sad one I wonder
will he make the news

3 > **You and Me**

You like to see me
wearing basketball shorts

I look at you and enjoy curvy
stripes across your chest

But we are really painting
a domestic banner together

Me, sitting on a sofa
papers strewn about us

There is even a white plastic
trash can, for target practice

In my heart, I want to create
a poem that is a poster of two

Moments when we watch
leaves dance outside the blinds

In our dining room with
a Chinese calendar next
to a psychedelic tapestry

And you like to cut napkins
in half while I blow my nose

I guess this will be a notebook
page of the daily times we share

We both like to drink from hot
mugs, you coffee and me tea

4 > **Tulare Trek**

Driving past golden hills

Then through the great agricultural valley

Smelling garlic and cows

Arrive at the city with two main streets

Every chain is there to choose from

First it's lunch Raising Canes

Check out dd's discounts, Dollar Tree, 99 store, CVS

Followed by Blaze Pizza dinner

Back to the 200 square foot square motel room

To watch some flat screen basketball

While charging the phones

Occasional voices outside the closed draped window

My wife giggles at a rubber pillow from Thailand video

I'm ready to endure a night in a white double bed

With my sweetie by my side providing leg on leg warmth

5 > **Sequoia Sojourn**

Gas up, hop on the freeway

Watch farmland become groves

Trees growing taller as the road winds

Feels like driving a sailboat through choppy waters

Signs declare narrow bridges, switchbacks, recent fires

An hour later reach the last space

In the closest parking and walk

Spot redwoods here and there increase in size

Down to the largest tree on Earth

Stranger couples take cellphone shots for each other

Stroll and find a double tree, a triple arbor

Look at the rings of a fallen giant

Thousands of years longer than a human life

Huff on stone steps back to the car

Sit on halved wood benches on the way

Then unwind the maze to return

Past homey hotels and restaurants

Homes with streams in their backyards

Arrive at the city to stay the night

Tomorrow morning retrace the highway home

6 > **Still Life**

On one edge of the dining table,
a clear plastic gallon bottle of
purified drinking water is flanked
by two somewhat unevenly used
cardboard paper towel tubes.

One is to the inside left, the other
right, looking like two supplementary
fuel tanks for an Artemis booster rocket.

When observed from directly above,
the combination kind of appears to be
like a dog's face, with the two tubes
as eyes, the bottle cap a nose, and
its handle the jowls and mouth.
I imagine it barking out, woof!

Day after day the bottle is slowly
being emptied, the towel sheets
torn off one by one, until eventually
the empty cylinders are tossed into
a white plastic recycling bucket.

Just need to replace both
to create table art again.

7 > **The Gap** (inspired by Tanya Ko Hong)

Between
America and China

Between
English and Chinese

Between
Facebook and WeChat

Between
Hello and Ni Hao

Between
Beautiful and Piaoliang

Between
Good Morning and Zaoshang Hao

Between
Morning Shower and Nighttime Shower

Between
Sharing Biology and Sharing Culture

Between
Independent and Communist

Between
Prepackaged Food and Cooking

Between
Ralphs and Great Wall

Between
Rock and Ballad

Between
Man and Woman

Between
Me and You

And yet
We make Us

Come together
Inside the Gap

8 > **Appreciation**

After attending a
super spreader pre-
Halloween poetry reading
maskless in a
black room with
no open windows,

we spend my
birthday week at
home, feverish, body
ached, sore throated,
congested and coughing.

Now I munch
on popcorn from
a white porcelain
bowl during the
writing time of
the online Saturday
workshop and hear

my wife in
the bathroom washing
clothes with the
portable spinner. I
walk down the
hallway to visit
her—she's naked.

I apologize, give
her body a
big wet hug.
Think to myself,
I'm feeling better.

9 > **Some Things to Do on This Planet**

After a sunny afternoon spent indoors critiquing poetry on Zoom with friends
My wife and I go to the thrift store to look for bookcases
but she finds coffee or tea cups with matching saucers blue striped half price
Then back home I enjoy a salad made by my life partner
Finally relax selecting music to listen to and post on Facebook
Done with that I stroll over to the bathroom to pee
Switch on the light, look into the toilet
I see a tiny dark floater
Must have been left behind by you-know-who
There's even a crumpled ball of tissue beside it
Wait a second, this ain't poop
Isn't that really a triangle on the surface
with two antennae twitching
It's a moth, soaked and suffering
I piss all over the little lake,
aiming for more indignity for the errant intruder and flush
An unpleasant way to end this stinking poem

10 > **In the World War III Museum**

Piles of melted steel, rubbled bricks, and scattered wood shards to walk around for hours

Shells of ships, planes, trucks, and cars to gaze at from an uncomfortable short distance

Shadows of humans, dogs, cats, even mice to be observed on walls and floors so close you can touch them

Videos of world leaders in disagreement, of people segregated in differently named countries and neighborhoods in this bunker

Finally, on these tables, mounds of cooked hair, scrapings of charred flesh, and chunks of fragmented bones as evidence we were all the same

11 > **Things to Remember Before the War**

a beach sunrise

a bird in a tree

a rainbow garden

butterflies

stained glass

live music

a swirling dress

a scraggly beard

a soccer ball

pet cat

a cup of tea

children's smiles

sunset skyline

poetry reading

a starry night without lights

12 > **From the Blue Bible, Onward...***

I encountered James Tate's taxonomy of tight twists
I enrolled in the Henri Coulette school of sweet soliloquies
I met Michael Shepler & saw short stuff is significant too
I ventured off into Marcielle Brandler's bashes of bountiful blues
I tutelaged under Jack Grapes' great gut-busting gustos
I overwhelmed to John Milton's murky mess of mellifluousness
I studied Emily Dickinson's daring dollops of denial
I copied Stephen Crane's creative classics of contrasts
I mimicked Gregory Corso's condemnation of conjugal captivity
I relived Gary Soto's storytelling of unsafe streets
My ears danced to Kamau Daaood's delightful discourses of days
I sought out Mike Carlin's home for hifalutin humor
I reveled rifling through Michele Serros sexy sibilant stories
I chanced upon Carl Stilwell's southern strategies for soirees
I glorified in Ellyn Maybe's masterful mullings of multitudes
I flocked to join Larry Jaffe's jovial jubilant joints
I pleasured in Rick Lupert's likeable lineage of LOL
I dog-eared Murray Thomas' tasty tomes of topography
I learned well from Laurel Ann Bogen's individual word emphasis
I devoured Jeffrey McDaniel's musing magic on mankind
I swooned at James Evert Jones' indigo intonations
I traveled inside Luis Javier Rodriguez's roads of rough remembrance
I joyed to Lois P. Jones' lines of long lusciousness
I riffed to Mike Sonksen's sacred sounds of cities
I dug Matt Sedillo's sonorous scathings of society
I amazed at Marvinlouis Dorsey's devastatingly deadly diatribes
I blew my mind with Alicia Viguer-Espert's expert enunciations of ecstasy
I found kinship inside Jackie Chou's catty collection of catastrophes
I lolled in Gregory Foster's (G.T.'s) fruitful funky foundation
I astounded to Coco's uncompromised unicorn creations
I marveled at Chuka Susan Chesney's prose of poetic particulars
I knelt for Traci Akemi Kato-kiriyama's kancer killing kollection
I sought a daily dose of Rich Ferguson's fun Facebook fonetics
Even my Alexis Rhone Fancher-like fantasy was filled as one of her fantastic fotos
Because of all these powerful poets for dedicated decades now
I have produced my own publishing palace for poesies

* Norton Anthology of Modern Poetry

1 > Your Precious Love (12 03 2022)
2 > It's All Too Much (12 04 2022)
3 > Imperfection (12 18 2022)
4 > Space Journeys (01 07 2023)
5 > Questions and Advice Derived from Jeff Beck titles (01 25 2023)
6 > Seventeen Years of Good Monterey Park Childhood Memories (01 25 2023)
7 > Can? (01 25 2023)
8 > C.A.T. (02 02 2023)
9 > Have You Ever... (02 04 2023)
10 > Driving Away Early Weekday (02 19 2023)
11 > No Seals in Seal Beach (02 19 2023)
12 > I'm Making Faces at Breakfast (02 19 2023)
13 > At the Huntington (02 19 2023)

1 > **Your Precious Love**

(Written in synergy with "Kiss Remix #2" by Richard May)

You are the butterfly

who fluttered onto my skin

made me feel the music

of lips on lips leading

to mouth into mouth dancing

dripped like Motown 45's

because Marvin Gaye had found

his Tammi Terrell

and as the Atlantic is rough

you flipped my lower finger

from torn conversation into

a collage of hot conversion

You have become my Queen of Hearts

inspiring me to create this wall of words

2 > **It's All Too Much**

A universe littered with galaxies beyond my imagination

Every spiral stretching outward festooned of stars

Each sun sporting some planets, moons and asteroids

This sphere always covered by untold clouds

Oceans alive since evolution evolved here

Thousands upon thousands of whales, sharks, and fish cruising currents

Shores infested in the billions because trees grow and humans manifest

Beings briefly bringing forth into being millions of buildings and books

Made merrier making music and art and children

A ground even more populated around a quadrillion animals and insects

Enough food and flowers to delight all those eyes and noses and mouths

Burgeoning brains recreate creating electric visions and revisions

I'm just a pixel in a pixel in a pixel in a pixel

Part of the whole shebang breathing in and out

Cosmic light went on, someday I am shut off

To be recycled as the planet pleases until it ceases

Also repurposed multiversally for unknowable time

Does God have a new design planned in the possibly etch-a-sketch future

3 > **Imperfection**

My nearly 30 year old daughter is an enhanced model.
You can find photos of her skin on Instagram.

My son has a braced drop foot. Hang on to yourself,
he's spending his 44th birthday Big Bear snowboarding.

This morning I pretended I was a horse, so my spouse
could slap my hindquarters repeatedly to make me whinny.

My wife has many cute freckles on her face, every day
she smooths a light wand over a coat of vanishing cream.

Now I'm meeting with you all eye to eye in a Zoom session.
What do you think of the finish of my newborn poem?

4 > **Space Journeys**

My mother kept
my earliest drawings
of Fireball XL5,
a rocket ship from
a television show
I don't remember.

A few years later,
I thrilled to Thunderbirds
human-like puppets
who awkwardly sauntered
to their numbered vehicles,
one even went underwater.

Then came the actual
NASA moon landing,
I became an at home
researcher who shared his
discoveries at school with
mimeos for my classmates.

But when I grew to an adult,
life gave me the opportunity
to get onto a rollercoaster,
screaming like my girlfriend
and vomiting not far from
the ride exit, end of dream.

5 > **Questions and Advice derived from Jeff Beck titles**

Will this Earthquake create
a Freeway Jam?

Can a Blue Wind
Live In The Dark?

Might the Darkness (Earth In Search Of A Sun)
be Rollin' And Tumblin'
like a Left Hook?

People Get Ready for
the Big Block,
Stand On It
or receive the Sling Shot!

We know Savoy
is here on Earth, but
Where Were You today?

I guess She's A Woman
who is neither a Scatterbrain
nor a Roy's Toy, right?

I Ain't Superstitious, yet
her Rice Pudding could make one
Throw Down A Line, maybe, possibly?

Goodbye Pork Pie Hat,
The Final Peace may be found
in a Corpus Christi Carol,
because Nessun Dorma
will leave us all so Serene.

6 > **Seventeen Years of Good Monterey Park Childhood Memories**

Wake up early Christmas morning to run to the living room to find lots of wrapped presents under the decorated live tree (at my sister Sue's request) in front of the red brick fireplace

My two door down friend John knocks on our front door on Holly Oak Drive summer mornings to play Legos with me and create a little Monterey Park complete with plastic tree-lined houses with Hot Wheels parked in the driveways and firework stands to hand drive to and a 12" black and white television as our hilltop bed drive-in (I once built a White House but only the front was white)

Race up the concrete ramps to shoot marbles in the paved curb around the edge of Hillcrest Elementary School's vast green grass playground

Also advantageous playing basketball left-handed on the asphalt rectangle lined with tether ball poles of that same playground

Become a shark and my sister a dolphin at the Garfield swim school near Riggin Street

Afternoons and weekends go outside into the street to pretend we were our Dodger and Ram heroes playing baseball with a tennis ball in which a home run was hitting it to be found in the front yard ivy of a down the street neighbor and vinyl football touchdowns were had when you streaked past a sidewalk light pole

Recall my mother kneading meatloaf adding ketchup or oven roasting grilled cheese sandwiches to eat from TV trays and my father frying French toast on Saturday mornings

Take a long walk down the Arroyo Drive hill with my cousin Mike on a hot afternoon to get a cola Slushy for 69 cents at the Stop 'N' Go on Potrero Grande Drive (and getting mine for free because I had no money and the clerk said go ahead and get one) and the happy return climb back up sipping on a red and white striped plastic straw

Delight in back patio Halloween birthday parties surrounded by elementary school friends in costumes captured in black and white then color Polaroid photos then trick or treat up and down the suburban streets when it got dark (extra candy for Bd-boy)

Ride my green Huffy bicycle behind Atlantic Square and find a new Boog Powell first baseman's left-handed glove lying in the alleyway

Surf the hills of south Monterey Park on my ram horn handlebar and sissy bar seat orange Sears bicycle to play basketball in friends' driveways where the metal hoop and wood backboard were mounted atop a garage door

Put another wishbone on the mantle high in the dining room every Thanksgiving spent with nuclear family full with turkey and stuffing and gravy and mashed potatoes and green peas and pumpkin pie for dessert

A family and friends barbecue at the Monroy's house with a succulent pig roasting in a hole in the backyard

Watch men walk on the moon for the first time in black and white on our 19" color television in the living room where we usually would lie on our stomachs to enjoy Saturday morning cartoons

Got to lecture at school about the moon landings with hand lettered mimeo question sheets I made to distribute to my fellow classmates and I won the class spelling bee too

Lie on my bed late at night to root for the Lakers on my 12" black and white teevee and record Midnight Special and Don Kirshner's Rock Concert acts with my Realistic portable cassette recorder hand-held microphone

Head a block over to Coriolanus Drive to visit Albert's house to audio tape our SC show (Sawano/Campbell) in his bedroom about music and Disneyland while his mother taught piano lessons in the living room

Walk hand in hand with my girlfriend Gaylin to her Ackley Street house to jump the backyard brick wall to hike the dirt road behind the Tikis where there were small ponds with tadpoles to catch with glass jars

After school at Garvey Junior High (where we played basketball on the asphalt courts before school, during recess and lunch, and after school) Ira and I trek up Garvey Avenue to buy six hot dogs for a dollar at Der Weinerschnitzel and RC Colas to drink on the Orange Avenue hill to home

Tammy and I design record covers together (me: On The Cover Of The Rolling Stone, her: Tie A Yellow Ribbon 'Round The Old Oak Tree) in 8th grade during art class on the second floor of the main building at Garvey Junior High on Jackson Avenue

My friends and I play the basketball card and dice game I created in my bedroom and at school I organize an unofficial one-on-one basketball tournament featuring my compiled stat sheets

Junior High friends dealing poker for money at the dining table in Bear's house on Ash Drive while Dark Side Of The Moon came out of the living room speakers

Ten speed bicycle down the Orange Avenue hill to the corner of Garvey and Garfield to shop at Clan Records where Tammy (soon to be Miss Monterey Park) worked

Win a turtle race at Barnes Park because my sister and I learned from losing that pointing your tortoise in the direction of the plunge makes them step briskly toward the splashing water

7 > **Can?**

Can a rock wait patiently to be broken again and again into other lives as pebbles, grains of sand?

Can a dog cross the rainbow bridge and find something on the other side?

Can a light bulb fret that it will one day cease to illuminate?

Can a human believe, when they die, they will be reincarnated as a rock?

Can a human believe, when they pass on, they will rejoin their dog in paradise?

Or are we all like light bulbs, unconscious in our recycling?

8 > **C.A.T.**

A dusty clipboard,
drink stained slate
with a couple chipped
corners, but the clip
retains a strong metal
spring, worn a groove

I added stickers
on the front surface,
Wile E Coyote next
to Road Runner

It was a gift from Tim,
my 3rd grade student
when I was an 8th grader
Cross Age Teaching

He also gave me
blue vinyl binders
from his father's
manufacturing job

Over the decades,
it has held poems
for my performances

50 years later,
I still have it

9 > **Have you ever...**

...tried using a key
instead of a quarter
to unlock an Aldi
shopping cart?

...shoplifted $1,000
of Legos from Target,
not for "family members",
but to sell?

...worked for Grubhub,
made a measly $6.69
on a delivery that
totalled $25.47?

...left a restaurant,
paying for your meal
on your way out, because
you didn't like your relatives?

...shot down a Chinese
spy balloon since that is
your job flying a fighter jet
from a Carolina air force base?

I have done none of these Google-able
things, yet I have been on the front page
of local 20th century newspapers twice,
once as a Barnes Park teenage turtle racer,

and again in the El Monte bus station
performing poetry in a safety jacket
to waiting riders about French toast,
street football, and spring love

10 > **Driving Away Early Weekday**

On a warming highway weaving along
rolling slopes and western shoreline

The Santa Barbara pier is open
for delivery trucks not a meal

So I engine my wife 43 more miles
to enjoy Belgian waffles alfresco

We walk the sunny sidewalks and shop
around flower planters and two windmills

Buy some Danish and chocolate fudge
and trudge back to the car to go home

Where I laughingly proclaim we traveled
128 miles just to have breakfast

Outside of our rented home to avoid
a single day of morning routine

11 > **No Seals in Seal Beach**

Drove our landlord and her husband
to the Long Beach cruise drop off

Then didn't want to just drive home so
I skirted coastal highway neighborhoods

To the familiar romantic pier where we
always stroll hand-in-hand and look out

At the Pacific Ocean rippling blue,
take cellphone photos of gliding seagulls,

And white wave breaks, palm trees
standing tall in the sun and wind

Walk by our favorite shops to capture
overpriced trinkets and potted flowers

Buy the Surfer's Special, two burritos and a soda
which we leisurely down on a sea-facing bench

With a bag of copious tostadas to later munch
back home for lunch before open door sex

12 > **I'm Making Faces at Breakfast**

with sliced in half buttered bun
atop a semi-circle of fried egg

with a bowl of lumpy oatmeal topped
with strategically placed nuts or raisins

with halved kiwi fruit eyes and
four arranged red grape smile

with a side-facing toast slice featuring
three dabs of almost melted butter

with apple wedges, peach pit nose,
and upturned mandarin section

with a pair of round dumplings and
facing cocoanut breaded shrimp

with pancake, waffle, or hash brown halves
over a salsa and cheese layered omelet

sometimes the folded white and yolk
looks like the United States or China

once battered fish sticks and a ketchup
mound became a score of 11 – 0

with butter-brushed beef buns
and a cut-up avocado in soy sauce

with two red grapes (again, love 'em)
and a daily Move Free capsule

with three or five well-placed chocolate
or cinnamon cookies on a round plate

I will use a fork or knife to replace
a missing eye or mouth, whatever it is

I try to portion it down to maintain
anthropomorphism as long as I can see it

13 > **At the Huntington**

First we go to the Chinese Garden to
act like we're taking an international trip,
stand in front of smile-roofed pavilions

Then walk down to the Japanese Garden
to capture some koi or bonsai, we photograph
a dining room as if we were kneeling adjacent

A stroll to the Australian Garden follows
allows photo-ops leaning near strange bulbous
trees and hairy knotty flowerless bushes

Head off to the Desert Garden to compare
the height of cacti to ourselves and notice
the communal patterns in which they grow

Next we're stepping up to the library where
guards watch us gaze upon early printed tomes
and handwritten speeches in glass cases

Finally to the two story home and art gallery
to view Pinky and Blue Boy and urns and
clocks and bronze sculptures, oh my

On our way out we pass stone busts
and intricate overdone fountains, even
enjoy flowered arbors in the parking lot

1 > UNO Party! (03 04 2023)
2 > To Thank You (03 06 2023)
3 > After the rain (03 06 2023)
4 > "The Joshua Parade" (03 19 2023)
5 > Alistair's Stare (03 19 2023)
6 > "Serious Cloud Bank" (03 19 2023)
7 > Dynamic Dawn (03 30 2023)
8 > Chile` (04 21 2023)
9 > Carrie the Cockroach (04 27 2023)
10 > Driveway Garden (04 27 2023)
11 > Sonnet for the Ekphrastic (05 06 2023)
12 > What better way to eat on Mother's Day… (05 14 2023)
13 > Living in a world time… (05 19 2023)
14 > W. I. F. E. (06 13 2023)
15 > I will never live in a world without cars (06 13 2023)

1 > **UNO Party!**

The muffins in the clear plastic
case on the dining table look
like butter and chocolate flowers

The cards my wife deals out
are red, yellow, green, and blue
like rectangular flowers

I gaze up at three birthday balloons
still tethered to the curio stand
naturally bunched like flowers

I turn to the open blind window
notice buds that will become lemons
sway because they are flowers

And my spouse is my favorite
flower to water, thinking this as
she sits and wins, munches and wins

I'm distracted, inspired to poetry,
so I lose the round like a wilted flower,
but gain a freshly budded poem

2 > **To Thank You**

I pull back the gauzy curtains

Step onto the white balcony

Hold on to a wooden post

Gaze upon the waves waving in

See the glorious sun setting

A few scattered clouds float like birds

Seagulls glide in the blue sky wind

And in the glowing distance

Oil tankers black silhouettes

Spoil the majestic view

Creating holes in the fabric

3 > **After the rain**

a partially soaked dry

leaf on the wet welcome mat

wants to come inside

4 > **"The Joshua Parade"**

Inspired by Alexis Rhone Fancher's photo

Could be an extended family
of four adults, three kids lagging,
marching off to visit relatives.
Yet they do not traipse at all,
except for the wind in their spires.
They are surrounded by like trees,
rooted in place, groups, individuals,
just like humans, save for faces
and fingers and legs to walk.
So they stay, living their positions
under the shiny blue desert sky,
attached to the soil of a vast planet,
dreaming of humanity, some day
hope to saunter into complicated lives.

5 > **Alistair's Stare**

One-year-old takes an inadvertent selfie
looking down into the cell phone seeing
what is up and around in a young world.
Baby blue pacifier complements his eyes,
secure the brick chimney is not a human,
for there is a hand holding a chair attached
to a familiar grandfather face with gray hair
above, with quizzical concerned expression.
All dominated by the white beamed ceiling
which is the fake sky in this room that hangs
a circular light unswitched and out of reach.
If only he could flip over, stand on the smooth
painted wood as a reverse god overseeing,
everything would still be beyond him for now.

6 > **"Serious Cloud Bank"**

Inspired by Alexis Rhone Fancher's photo

A fluffy white swath has grown
like a moist wall towering over all
humans can muster to build below:
tiny bridges, buildings, freeways.
Cars, mere toys carrying itsy bitsy
creations navigating a designed world.
The massive cloud covers everything,
temporarily blinds drivers to use wipers,
as the behemoth passes through, crying,
leaving tears everywhere, on every ounce
of concrete and rubber and glass, sinking
in to surrounding soil, ready to reincarnate
as small lives turning green, being eaten,
infesting, investing in becoming again.

7 > **Dynamic Dawn**

Up in pastel blue
sky clouds swarm and
turn around each other,
cause frayed rolling edges.

Unseen sun below is
a dragon breathing orange
into warring nimbus strands.
On the surface, palm

trees and power poles
reach high but don't
communicate with cool air.
It's the opposite, wind

invisibly swirls through wires
and fronds. At street
level, silent road cracks
and ages under daily

heating and movement down
into darkness. Eyes close,
wait for next morning's
display. What shall we

sight tomorrow? Traipse on
to gaze horizon where
creatures conjure models that
shadow imitate massive nature.

8 > **Chile`**

We bought
extremely delicious
High Flavor
Candy Hearts
red grapes
from Chile`
at Costco

I listen
to a
hard rocking
instrumental band
called Octopus
from Chile`
on YouTube

Look on
my cellphone
recall it's
near Argentina
Too bad
I'll never
go there

I guess
I don't
have to
I can
experience Chile`
from here
Thanks trade

9 > **Carrie the Cockroach**

I was born inside a wall
Surrounded by brothers and sisters
We eat crumbs and drink puddles

Then a terrible rumbling comes
The walls break open
Smoke enters every crevice

We choke to breathe the ash
We wander searching
We run out of crumbs

Only chunks of flesh
There are no more puddles
Except dried blood

A week goes by
So thirsty
A month food gone

Now we
The survivors
Are wreckage too

10 > **Driveway Garden**

trumpets of white calla lilies

row of spires of green onion stalks

clusters of purple suns, pink suns

succulent heads with long stubbly necks

yellow "tree" flower rises off the same stem

weed push-thru concrete crack circle

birds of paradise crane spiky orange "hair"

glasses-wearing poet observes outside barred house

11 > **Sonnet for the Ekphrastic**

When the penis fit the fucking hole
We decided to put on golden rings
Live in a rectangular box together
Hold hands until we become spirits
Watch the sun rise and set every day
Wait for the urge to mate to return
It always does in at least one of us
So we couple and uncouple an hour
Go back to the need of sundry things
Wash up, brush up, cook up, eat up
See the golden glow on our faces
Laugh over emerging lines and spots
Words unspoken say more about two
Than anything this poet can assemble

12 > **What better thing to eat on Mother's Day than organic eggs**

for buttered French toast
with syrup all made
from underpaid labor

and nuts and grapes
and raisins and oranges
arduously picked from trees

and mango juice bought
from an outlet store
run by a woman

my wife rouses from bed
to find a man who loves her
cooked breakfast because of she

13 > Living in a world time
That occasionally rhymes

Where you learn easily
To love a familial entity
Much bigger than you
Who picks you up and
Holds you tenderly

You become larger
Until the day comes
When you step and wait
To live on a planet
Where you try to equate

Ultimately the hour rounds
Where around you watch
The frail exist bedbound
As seconds tick
Breaths faint sound

Then release from hell
Into a non-existent spell
A plane where life develops
Mouth, ears, eyes in shell
That turns and rots well

Feeds the ground gain
Where new creatures
Work along the chain
To reach the moment of
Inhale again and again

Where intake of water, milk
Apples, oranges, bananas
Rice, noodles, buns, fun
Hugs, kisses, copulation
Nurture self-replication

All made possible where fraught
The gift of movement
Language and thought
Examination of being sought
Implements innate desires

14 > **W. I. F. E.**

Pretty lady in Wendy's munches French fries one by one and looks out the plate glass windows with smoky big sunglasses perched above her forehead

Frame arms tucked into the waterfall of her long straight smooth silky black hair raised a little by a small tortoise shell colored spider clip

She's wearing a slim black stretchy fabric unzipped black jacket (with Hurley printed in white down the left sleeve) to reveal a line of cleavage dividing the smiling edge of her black low-cut tee shirt

A stylish stripe stitched Nautica embossed between two lines black cellphone purse is slung over one shoulder to lay on her lap

Where tight black jeans conform to her legs and end with new shiny black vinyl low-rise boots whose rubber heels rest on the restaurant high stool tiny brass bar footrest

15 > **I will never live in a world without cars**

My wife didn't feel like cooking tonight because she hurt her pinky playing basketball with me at the park in the morning

So we stopped shooting and I drove her to the nearby Ross to shop for cool clothes since it was Senior Tuesday

While we were waiting in line I saw an old girlfriend in the next aisle looking at merchandise

I immediately turned and said nothing

Here we are now at the Wendy's where my ex-wife liked to dispense Diet Dr. Pepper from the self-serve machine

I drink the same formula and look out the windows at autos passing briskly to get home

Maybe we should go too

1 > She lives in a world of noise (06 16 2023)
2 > Terrestrial (06 17 2023)
3 > Father's Day Morning Stroll (06 17 2023)
4 > I love to sniff the world (06 19 2023)
5 > Blind (06 20 2023)
6 > Instant Crush (06 23 2023)
7 > Huntington Drive (06 24 2023)
8 > Simile City (07 03 2023)
9 > The Adventures of Bao Bao and Dog Dog (07 04 2023)
10 > Big Family on a Corner (07 06 2023)
11 > Ars Dogma (07 07 2023)
12 > Scene from Edgewood Drive (07 16 2023)
13 > Sunset (07 23 2023)
14 > Sky whispers (07 26 2023)
15 > Skunk and Seal (08 01 2023)
16 > Real Love (08 17 2023)
17 > Sonnet to Oblivion (08 31 2023)

1 > **She lives in a world of noise**

In the middle of the quiet night
She hears footsteps to the bathroom
It's late and she's sleepy

In the morning she senses
Doors opening and window
Shades scrolled up and open

Then comes cooking sounds
Click click of activated stove
Sizzling wok, stirring wand

Welcome odors arrive to table
She lifts herself, saunters over
To get near the meat content

A few bites of human food
She heads to the aluminum
Plate of kibble she knocks into

Laps water from a proximate tray
It is time for a walk outside
Swinging of iron gated entry

Paws on the concrete driveway
Occasional passing car
Distant construction bangs

Across the street one smells
She barks back in response to this
Sighted fenced canine protecting

After whizzing on grass lawn
Grandma's boots jogging in alley
She sniffs patch, inspired to squat

The crinkling of plastic bag
The closing of trash bin
The resumption of trotting

The tug of the leash helps
But she knows instinctively to
Step on familiar smooth floor

She turns and turns in a circle
To lie on her beloved bed
Proceeds to lick herself clean

Sometimes nibbling too well
Removing a tuft of fur because
She misses her vacationing master

If we go out without her
Sukie can hear the inserted key
And wake up from a nap

2 > **Terrestrial**

Thanks for the sun setting
How the red aura settles
On the dark mountain range

And far below the silhouettes
Of buildings lit with signs
And traffic lights multiplicity

Closer still homes rest on
Their concrete foundations
Supported by packed earth

And cars in the driveways
Also parked by the curbs
And sidewalks between them

A woman walks her dog
A man steps into his vehicle
Each their separate ways

Then the cracks in the street
The cooling air flowing
Over all, over all, over all

3 > **Father's Day Morning Stroll**

A mourning dove coos for a partner
Who flies to the branch above to meet
Together quiet in the tree for awhile

One squirrel chases another up
And down the trunk and around
They scurry off to the next arbor

Husband and wife walk their dog
Over sidewalk and alley to spend
Cool fresh time in such company

4 > **I love to sniff the world**

I put my nose to the ground
There I have found the odors
I seek in my day's existence

I need to whiff the concrete
Looking for traces of you
Where you last did pee

I usually detect you around
Clumps of grass smelling
Much like what came out

Then I am compelled to
Take a nibble of remnants
You left behind for me

My master doesn't approve
But understands it's my
Nature to take and give

Something for you too
To Inhale my sweetness
Exited from the same hole

The universal messages
We send to each other
Just to say I think of you

Even though we haven't
Met I know you smell so
Good you inspire me

5 > **Blind**

If I couldn't see
I'd be playing
Pinball with the
Sidewalk too

And I would feel
Every bump
Each dip in
The concrete

I'll hear birds
Chirping above
The close whoosh
Of passing cars

Feel cool wind
Rushing over
My moving body
In the morning

I guess I would
Learn my favorite
Sense would be
To smell all

The concrete
The grass
The urine
The exhaust

And the air
Between everything
Will always be
The best sensation

6 > **Instant Crush**

step
in your shoes
on a sidewalk
ant

take your sandal
in your hand and smash
a spider perched
on a tiled shower wall

walk into
a car crusher
and sit
down

fly a helicopter
or plane at
full speed into a hillside
or tall building

climb into
an uncertified submersible
and descend to
10,000 feet

7 > **Huntington Drive**

Bushy trees like
giant broccoli

Pointed tall
pines undermatched
across the street
by church steeple

Towering palms
on side of road
sway like pom poms
over elementary school
on opposite side

8 > **Simile City**

A family of red roses
Cluster together
Like a solar array

A pair of parrots
Screech overhead
Like pod racers

Two honking cars
Pass in parking lot
Like dogs barking

Air conditioners
Hang out windows
Like bored citizens

A couple walk their
Pooch on the sidewalk
Vanish like settlers

9 > **The Adventures of Bao Bao and Dog Dog**

She thinks we walk with a purpose
To release internal fluids and solids
This may be true, but there is
A higher inspiration: to inspire
Through the nostrils the scents
Of the sidewalk, the lawns, the world
That is the real pleasure, to appreciate
What humans cannot or will not
Focus on, the subtle joys of sniffing
Traces of urine and poopilage
Even flowers and weeds have essence
Yet, just standing in the wind
Might be the ultimate ecstasy
To feel cool air itself caress hair
Then return home to lap up water
Munch on kibble or wet food
Start the healthy cycle again
But first a thorough licking clean
Followed by a nice nap on my bed

10 > **Big Family on a Corner**

Got a big screen TV today, stowed
the big cardboard box in the back of
their curb parked big black pickup truck

Couldn't fit it in the wide driveway,
there's already four big SUV's side-by-side
crowding the slightly cracked concrete

The big sideyard tent top is still up, nearby
are the black plastic tubes of mortars
that were fired during the big Fourth holiday

Four color coded trash bins have been
set out at the curb, overfilled with stuff
like any other multigenerational group

We keep walking the dog by because
they've got seven cameras perched
on the corners of their old house

Sometimes we see a white cat sitting
on a windowsill, but no more, two big
new air conditioners occupy sills now

Yesterday they had their little bulldog off
a leash, he barked and sniffed the behind
of blind Sukie until he was slapped away

They gently apologized and went on with
their familial activities; on a later walk tonight,
we just heard the television as we passed

11 > **Ars Dogma**

Stop and smell the grass
That's my motto

Wait and feel the air
The ways to be alive

Let the afternoon pass
What's the rush to go home

When you've got driveway
And sidewalk to saunter

You can be a dog even
If you only have two legs

So traipse back indoors
Because you want to

Go lap up some water
Nibble some kibble

Clean up tongue style
Finish with a good nap

Then rinse repeat retrace
Those steps you made before

What a life for a canine
Or any size being living

12 > **Scene from Edgewood Drive**

An airplane crosses the sky

Irregular skyline on the horizon

Flowers near cars parked in driveways

A man sweeps the sidewalk

A woman walks her dog

An SUV passes briskly by

The hot dog stand is not open

Aftermath of a kid's birthday party

Trash bins lined up at the curb

Sun bakes edifice of new storage building

No train on the tracks below

Cross the street if you see someone

Everyone wrapped up in their own lives

A mourning dove hoo hoos out of sight

13 > **Sunset**

because I saw a bright glow coming
from between the window blinds
I stepped out of my rented house

looked to the sky and envisioned
brilliant yellow ragged ram's horns
of lit up cloud formations arresting

like two raised arms over the Earth
below they widened until they were
spread out like crab claws beneath

the sky crustacean an orange ocean
skirting the tree lined silhouette
horizon which led my eyes westward

to unseen millions of unknown souls
who no doubt if they were outside
took mental notes or cell phone

photos to share with the ephemeral
moving feed of creation itself
switched on not just for hue man

14 > **Sky whispers**

Wake up my eyes, clouds in the air,
Like trees reach out try to touch moisture

Clouds in the welkin dance with love
Like white dragons or flapping doves

Me and the trees can only watch and sway
Want generated winds to carry us away

Clouds stretch and become so wispy
Spirits in the baby blue get so hot and dry

Trees are a feeling audience and so am I
Some clouds finger God because they are

So fleeting, so temporary, so repetitive there
One day they are this, they know they can fly

The next they are not, I too wish and cry
Eat me ground, process me, send me high

15 > **Skunk and Seal**

in the middle of the full moon night
Sukie barks at something passing by
seconds later spray smell permeates
the house but we are sleepy we wake
up in the morning to pervasive stench
put the dog in the backyard and go
out for breakfast, no, not locally, no,
I need beach air to clear my nostrils
so we soar down the freeway to Seal
where we can relive our romantic meals
walk on the pier take photos stroll back
to a favorite spot for me the Garden
Shop to enjoy colorful flowers while
a monarch feeds on a Matilija poppy
what a capture still we must return to
our rented non-air-conditioned home
make sure doggie's okay and fed wash
off the wet pattern left on the screen
door by the frightened skunk who
passed won't venture this path again
we'll keep both portals shut run fans
dream in the bliss of a cool memory
on a hot midsummer August day

16 > **Real Love**

I seek you like a plane crossing the sky
I desire you like a flower sprouting out of the ground
I need you like a branch pushes through a wood fence
I wait for you like a parked SUV sits all day
I think of you like leaves on a tree dancing with the wind
I worship you like a pooch sniffing a verdant corner
I'm ready for you like a car starting up in the morning
I follow you like a dog walking on a leash behind you
I salute you like a flag waving with the breeze
I revel in you like a sun setting on the horizon
I miss you like two hounds barking behind a fence
I remember our times like distant traffic whooshing away

1 > Sonnet to Oblivion (08 31 2023)
2 > Pick Up Walk (09 02 2023)
3 > Mark (09 20 2023)
4 > I'm Satisfied If I Die Tonight (09 27 2023)
5 > Morning for the Dead (10 18 2023)
6 > Now I'm 64 (10 31 2023)
7 > Walking Through a Graveyard (11 04 2023)
8 > A Poem Is (11 25 2023)
9 > The sun rose this morning (12 08 2023)
10 > Faces and Flowers (12 09 2023)
11 > Mina (12 11 2023)
12 > The pantoum rose this morning (12 13 2023)
13 > Pantoum to Oblivion (12 13 2023)

1 > **Sonnet to Oblivion**

Where the moon is full
I cannot bark at any one
I blindly stare at heaven
See trees worship sun light
Even though it is mid night
A glow glints on every thing
Distant waves glimmer again
And again I am awe struck
The sand of the land walk
Tells me I am not alone
In this moment silent fall
When a life only wishes
There will be time to flee
To the bliss of unbeing

2 > **Pick Up Walk**

Even though the dog we sat
has been gone for a week
I don't want to lose the habit

So I tell my wife let's stroll
despite being animal-less
look at the morning moon

We retrace a familiar path
the street we've known
for five cohabitating years

Only this time we stumble
upon a menagerie of toys
strewn on a green verge

There's a smiling pink whale
an assortment of tea cups
scattered miniature road signs

Among other smaller objects
tiny flatbed cargo trucks
and faux medicine applicators

I stop and contemplate why
they are there so jumbled
Were they left in haste

We continue our sojourn
and sight the usual succulents
that look like green flowers

A knotted tree makes great
photography except in color
Mockingbird remembered

A sidewalk corner sports
a spray painted black X with
two red circles like angry eyes

My love says see the plane
encountering some clouds
it is circling around okay

But my mind cannot leave
the collection of children's
discarded happy plastic

When we return I postulate
if they are abuse victims
I hope both are safe now

What can we do but incant
my wish for no violence
by pilfering one favorite

To take home and gaze
upon to remind myself
we all need some magic

Just to successfully go
through each diurnal
in a world of humans

Who can become forgetful
that small creations do
help us plan our lives

Which depend on others
to either support or break
the dreams of futures

3 > **Mark**

We met fighting in a kindergarten sandbox for space
Became elementary friends a couple years later
But junior high is when our adventures blossomed
Walking home from school together splitting
Six Weinerschnitzel hot dogs for a dollar on the way
Up the hill to our tract home asphalt street lives
Punched you in your brace-filled mouth when you took my seat
The principal couldn't understand why buddies fight
Even the school play we were in Then And Now
Ended with real stage swings surfer vs chicano
You wrote me a letter telling me you were gay
Before revealing it to your family yet I knew
Already because you never talked about girls
I went to your bar mitzvah soon afterward
Next summer I stayed at your new home in Van Nuys
So I could go to Grant High to study typing
We had our greatest discoveries then in sexuality
We skinny dipped in your pool then streaked on the sidewalk
You introduced me to the progressive music of ELP
You were especially moved by the lyric on six million jews
We went to Yes concerts annually both of us big fans
You were my best man in my only courthouse wedding
Decades on we went to a small band show (who was it)
And you got mad at me for talking to a rocker girl
So you broke up with cisgender me completely
Then your father died and you invited me to the funeral
I didn't go just kept on being a Facebook friend
Learned how heartbroken you were when your dog passed
Found out you were hospitalized with kidney trouble
Now second hand I discover you've been gone for a year
What to make of this lifelong odyssey of memories
Of times when our hearts intersected in common interest
And moved on when we didn't fit any more
Fare well in that recycling earth love your ex-bestie

4 > **I'm Satisfied If I Die Tonight**

I've seen the sun rise to light a cloud-filled sky
Orange and pink like a bouquet of fresh roses

I've watched my babies being born like miracles
Soft crown, active limbs emerging out of hairy hole

I've ingested every one of my favorite dishes
From French toast bubbling like a blanket of Fall

To a diapered infant, I mean, a potato burrito
And my wife's seven ingredient fried rice

I've lived at least three different cultures though
Four marriages died from infidelity or neglect

Oh, I've had my share of hugs, kisses, licks, orgasms
They've kept me healthy enough to imitate otters

I've enjoyed music, movies, and most of all poetry
Which gave my life a soundtrack and written context

Now as I gaze at the coming sunset from my rented
Alhambra home I understand breaths are limited

And merely relish sounds and sights and tastes
Like a train passing, the curves of naked women

May I hold onto my beloved memories until I have
To let go, exhausted by this plentifulness of experience

5 > **Morning for the Dead**

A procession of black umbrellas across a grassy valley
To the peaked memorial mountain where a gold cross
Shines in fiery light as birds file over corpsed graves
Extended to silently reach for remembrance of illusory
Mourning in which some still believe geography divides
When we are all the same detritus feeding the ground
Only one red-covered mourner acknowledges he follows
This sad pack, observes their breathing for passing hours
The dynamic daily destruction that doesn't need our help
We are decorated finite presences on bountiful rich land
Today he will tell them time is just a perceived measure
For a flock who forgets they merely move moments since
Nothing else waits but lives on for perpetuated endings
Filled fallow minds finally comprehending the merger

6 > **Now I'm 64**

1

The first time
Death knocked
I rode a bicycle
No hands into
A white pickup

Got up from that
Walked my bike
Home with a friend
To find a worried
Mama and driver

The dark sun
On my forehead
Was obvious
At elementary
For two weeks

2

The second time
I flipped my ten speed
In front of a 60
Freeway onramp
Quickly righted

Headed for the curb
Touched my hair
A little blood
Oozing from my
Aching cranium

So I wheeled on
Not saying a word
About my slight
Misfortune before
Approaching tires

3

The third time
I was bodysurfing
at Brookhurst Beach
A six foot wave
Sent me to the sand

I looked at my leg
My knee cap outside
My joint--scream!
A lifeguard ran to me
Assured, you'll get drugs

After the dune buggy
Ride to Hoag Memorial
I lay down on back seat
As my teen buddy drove
My Horizon into a BMW

4

The fourth time in
My Toyota I attempted
To pass another only
She turned left into
The three of us

I spun the wheel
As fast as I could
Her sedan went
Over the side
Into a grassy ditch

The police came
Told me to drive
To the station
File a report in
No-fault Arizona

5

The fifth time
I opened the door
To take my son
To school and
The ground shook

The street undulated
Light poles swayed
We went anyway
Principal said go
No class today

I missed my 8 AM
Medical appointment
At Cal State LA where
A concrete slab of
Garage killed a woman

6

The sixth time
I was stopped
At a red light
In my new fire
Engine red pickup

A carful of
Teenagers in
A green Impala
Plowed into
My tailgate

They took off
I raced after them
Running through
Stop signs and
Failed to catch...

7

The seventh time
I was playing
Basketball at CSULA
My defense good
Even at old 40

One young collegian
Didn't like that
Passed the ball
Hard into my face
I crumpled slowly

Like a felled tree
Flat on my back
My glasses astray
I tried to get up
Couldn't for 20 min

8

The eighth time
I was on vacation
In San Jose on
The freeway going
To a poetry reading

In the exit lane
My girlfriend and I
Felt a sudden bang
I jumped out of
My rear-ended Cube

Found a beat up
White pickup with
A dazed man inside
The arriving officer
Said get in your car

9

The ninth time
I missed dying
I used to frequent
A dance studio
Because of girlfriends

One loved dancing
The other worked
There, I gave rides
To the owner's wife
For Andrew Jacksons

Years later when
I surfed the internet
I learned 11 were dead
And worried if it was
Someone I knew

10

Just last week
I entered a 7/11
At 5:30 AM
To buy a lottery
Ticket from the clerk

He said it was
Too early, the machine
Wouldn't let him
Login until 6
So I pondered

Staying to buy
Or driving back
To my sleeping
Wife, in bed I read
Of the 5:37 robbery

7 > **Walking Through a Graveyard**

Most plaques lie flat on ground or wall
A smattering of very old raised headstones
Looking closely at dates
Some babies lived as long as butterflies
Here are a father and a son who died on the same day,
must have been a car accident
Several double plots with quite a few plates
inscribed Beloved Husband and Wife
Sometimes one side doesn't have the information
filled out yet
We walk around the markers
Marvel at the variety of lifespans
Driving away from the mission
I feel like letting the speeders pass
So I can cherish the sunlight streaming through
the window warming my skin
And glance at all the scattered manuments
we leave behind for someone new to move into

8 > **A Poem Is**

"A poem is a house"
--Linda Ravenswood

A poem is a birth
Something here
Was not before

A poem is a hand
Guiding you
To revelation

A poem is a car
Transports you to
Another time place

A poem is a lover
Embraces your mind
Unforgettable shapes

A poem is a sky
Gaze into seemingly
Endless imagination

A poem is a tree
It stands there
Magnificent

A poem is a bird
Flies into your life
Perches in your soul

A poem is a donut
A great indulgence
Leaves you satisfied

A poem is a bed
Fall pleasantly asleep
Dream the feeling

A poem is a grave
Here lie thoughts
Of an knowable poet

9 > **The sun rose this morning**

Actually the earth turned
And here we are again
Those of us who got through
Another diurnal day and night
Can you still walk like a human
Can you still talk like a being
Do you hear breakfast cooking
Do you feel the air's chill
Well then you've come this far
And what do you have to show
Maybe a job, house, marriage, kids
If you're gifted you could be
Making some art, music, poetry
Thank the muses we made up

10 > **Faces and Flowers**

faces like flowers
you see them everywhere
some fully blossomed

flowers like faces
looking up or down
who ponders who

like faces flowers
have a countenance
you can read easily

like flowers faces
react to their environment
sicken and die

flowers faces like
are robust and
full of character

faces flowers like
are cultivated plants
reaping beauty

11 > **Mina**

When we are going outside
She makes up her face
In a mirror facing a window

She puts an outfit on
Usually tight and black to hide
And accentuate curves

Closing the door walking down
The driveway her hand reaches
For mine as we walk to the car

Always keeps a towel on the seat
To help my Cube seem new
She likes to sing while we travel

She enjoys shopping for food
To add vegetables and peppers
As spice in our noodles or rice

Tuesday morning is fun for us
Because it's senior day at Ross
She finds bargain designer duds

I like to surprise her with a weekend
Excursion to break monotony
This time Long Beach thrift stores

Clothes are her first priority
A nice purse and a pair of boots
A lucky discovery a collectable doll

After a long afternoon out
Home for dinner and conversation
She shows me videos of China

At night under the covers
Her toes touch my toes
With a special kind of love

12 > **The pantoum rose this morning**

Actually the earth turned
And here we are again
Those of us who got through
Another diurnal day and night

And here we are again
Can you still walk like a human
Another diurnal day and night
Can you still talk like a being

Will you still walk like a human
Do you hear breakfast cooking
Will you still talk like a being
Do you feel the air's chill

If you hear breakfast cooking
Well then you've come this far
If you feel the air's chill
What do you have to show

Well then you've come this far
Maybe a job, house, marriage, kids
What do you have to show
If you're gifted you could have

Maybe a job, house, marriage, kids
Making some art, music, poetry
If you're gifted you could be
Thanking the muses we made up

Making some art, music, poetry
Those of us who got through
Thank the muses we made up
The earth actually turned

13 > **Pantoum to Oblivion**

Where the moon is full
I cannot bark at any one
I blindly stare at heaven
See trees worship sun light

I cannot bark at any one
Even though it is mid night
See trees worship sun light
A glow glints on every thing

Even though it is mid night
Distant waves glimmer again
A glow glints on every thing
And again I am awe struck

Distant waves glimmer again
The sand of the land walk
And again I am awe struck
Tells me I am not alone

The sand of the land walk
In this moment silent fall
Tells me I am not alone
When a life only wishes

In this moment silent fall
There will be time to flee
When a life only wishes
To the bliss of unbeing

There will be time to flee
I blindly stare at heaven
To the bliss of unbeing
Where the moon is full

1 > God (12 20 2023)
2 > Opposites Find Commonality (12 22 2023)
3 > How Can a World (12 25 2023)
4 > Xmas (12 25 2023)
5 > Beyond Mammal (01 03 2024)
6 > When I Die (01 03 2024)
7 > Just (01 03 2024)
8 > Ask (01 03 2024)
9 > Woke Up (01 04 2024)
10 > Sun Set (01 07 2024)
11 > Sighting (01 08 2024)
12 > Baby Talk (01 11 2024)
13 > Metaphor Poets (01 16 2024)

1 > **God**

He's looking a bit worried
Gazes out at humanity disgusted
Why are you judging each other by color
Why do you label a life with one word
Here in the light everything is black and white
And brown and green and several more shades
The lines on his face display the decades
Of moving through this brilliant world
Only to find evil thoughts beside good
We are all made up of what you can see
And what you cannot is divine, a spirit
Which propels forward existence to an end
Where you will meet him simply as energy
The two finally bonded without argument
To create something new from detritus of old

2 > **Opposites Find Commonality**

We were two kindergarteners in the sandbox
We fought over using the same toy and space
The teacher separated us into respective corners
A couple years later we were fast friends
Each enjoying our square dance class
As junior high preteens we bonded over music
Still we fought one day over a single seat
I punched him on his brace-filled mouth
We both ended up a little bloody because of that
The principal said, how can these buddies fight
From then on we were concert going pals
Except for the occasional disagreement
About my not paying enough attention to him
He came out to me but I already knew
Spent too much time with a woman once at a show
So he broke off our lifelong friendship
A few years later he invited me to his father's funeral
I didn't go because I was tired of the drama
He died not very long after that of kidney failure
Did I forget to mention I was Catholic and
He was Jewish, probably since it didn't matter
To us it was a mutual interest that kept us
From fighting much to share our love of Yes
Maybe we can all learn something in this story

3 > **How Can a World**

with a warm and brilliant sunrise
with a sun shaped floor heater
with toasty puffy jacket over my sweats
with a hot oatmeal and vegetable omelet
sporting a cheddar cheese heart
with cellphone music by Sun Q
with my wife hanging wet clothes to dry outside
with Facebook friends offering Xmas wishes
ever end
easy
especially if this was Gaza, Israel
but it's not, it's Alhambra, California
so we live on for another day
with peace here but not there
with hope that will change
into tranquility everywhere
not just in most places

4 > **Xmas**

if this was 1963
I'd be excitedly getting up early
to run into the living room
to unwrap a (surprise!) Tonka jeep
and hand drive around the house

if this was 1968
I'd wake smiling in expectation
open the front door
take out a new banana seat bicycle
to explore the city

if this was 1973
I'd please my ears in bed
with the sound of 93 KHJ
then dig Chicago
on my gifted record player

if this was 1978
I'd slowly lift my lids
hearing the week-old baby
boy needs a diaper change
on the door held by sawhorses table

if this was 1983
I'd awaken next to my second wife
enjoy my two-week vacation
from teaching junior high school
happy my favorite band Yes is #1

if this was 1993
I'd gaze at my third wife and infant daughter
pour myself some cereal
watch the Lakers struggle without Magic
and write a poem about it

if this was 2013
I'd blink and wonder beside my fourth wife
if coming will be a peaceful year
with my fresh MFA on the wall
and the memory of a day in jail behind me

if this was 2017
I'd arise alone in my bedroom while
my fifth wife in our fifth day of marriage
stays celibate in her own room
as I contemplate a fast divorce

thank god this is 2023
I rouse and hug my sixth wife a good long time
thankful she will make me a hot breakfast
and the only price I have to pay
is washing the dishes afterward

5 > **Beyond Mammal**

Open my eyes
Sniff a little snot
Fist over mouth
Cough away phlegm
Let flatulence rip
Feel a change come
Stroke erect skin
Think of doing
The animal act
Of repetition
To elicit fluid
But she's asleep
Wait until morning
See if it occurs again
The urge to move
Beastly grunts
Followed by roar
Then clean up
With invented
Creature's comforts
Shower brush
Dress talk
Breakfast together
Sausage and eggs
Much better than
Alone wolf's life
Slip on shoes
Walk to SUV
Drive off to buy
More feathers
For the nest
How about a toy
Or two hours
Seated in culture
Time for dinner
Return home
Flex in bathroom
Nice to be retired
Lie down once more
Leg over leg
Repeat and rinse
Sleep like hamsters

6 > **When I Die**

don't feel sad
for me or miss me

because 75% of my body
evaporates up a chimney

soon in the clouds
ready to rain down on

the remaining 25%
tossed over the ground

become fertilizer for
newborn plants and trees

I will grow to feed
small creatures

and reanimate as
their children

See you later
in my next guise

reincarnated poet
re-experiencing

food chain
once again

7 > **Just**

Ask the ground
how it feels to be
rained over
stepped across

Question a plant
how chilly it is
when sun shines
on leaves and stem

Query small
creatures what
fear is like
or happiness

Interrogate a human
who decides
which beings
live or die

Inquire with
your god(s)
whether it was
their idea

Then posit
if all creation
is sentient and
part of you

8 > **Ask**

The wind the
exergies relating
to blowing or not

The clouds about
their weekly ride
on the jet stream

The land if all its
movement can
be beneficial

The ocean whether
going to and fro
achieves anything

The sky why
encompassing a globe
has purpose

The sun how blazing
a few billion years
will end up

The universe patiently
on the subject of
eventual lights out

The gods what
happens when there is
no one left to worship

9 > **Woke Up**

Able to see
Our bedroom in
The dark again

I could feel
Your warmth
Beside me

I inhaled
The scent
Of your skin

I kissed
Reverentially
Your cheek

I heard you
Make a slight
Enquiring sound

Moved in
For the loving
Endorphin hug

And it's only
Four a.m., thank
You nightlight

10 > **Sun Set**

The sky is on fire
A wall of orange
A blanket of gray atop
Cloud mass leaking like
A lava flow in the air

Light pierces through
A fissure, a force
Turns the whole nimbus
Into rosy puffs of fluff
Then the orb dips down

Below the dark horizon
A line of separation
Between silhouetted edges
And clouds becoming night
The canvas is now black

11 > **Sighting**

A skyscraper in my bedroom
Doesn't tell time like a bank building
But it does read temperature
At the top in green numerals
While providing exact degrees of heat

It towers over the clock radio
Which looks like a Disney Monsanto house
Except for the segmented digital readout
Signifying precise hour and minute
In a still dark room at night

One stands and one sits
Atop a much larger rectangle
Chunky like a Star Wars robot
Since it does double duty working
As a dresser and a nightstand

Where I can place my lenses
When I close my eyes to sleep
And dream of a city surrounding me
Inside this stucco wooden box
One of many on an infested planet

12 > **Baby Talk**

Bao Be is Chinese for baby
when I first wanted to call Mina
by an affectionate nickname

Bao By combines Chinese and English
reflecting our two language relationship
still sweet as a baby in any dialect

Bao Bao, okay, I like the sound
and repeat it like a baby in my love
for Aihua, that is her real name

Baby Bao Bao, yes, having been married
for over a year I regressed to baby
talk to capture the duality of it all

Bao Bao Bao is what I've been singing
lately to songs to make them about
my wife of nearly two years, Aihua Gao

13 > **Metaphor Poets**

Chaucer is my saucer
Shakespeare is my beer
Basho is my bro
Milton is my hilton
Pope is my dope
Blake is my lake
Shelley is my valley
Keats is my meats
Poe is my joe
Whitman is my man
Dickinson is my sun
Crane is my plane
Eliot is my chariot
Williams is my millions
Millay is my bay
Sandburg is my burg
Hughes is my blues
Thomas is my promise
Bishop is my worship
Frost is my cost
Swenson is my bon bon
Ginsberg is my iceberg
Corso is my torso
Plath is my path
Neruda is my barracuda
Bukowski is my ski
Angelou is my beau
Tate is my date
Maybe is my gravy
Serros is my pharoahs
Hong is my bong
Kingfisher is a wisher

www.ingramcontent.com/pod-product-compliance
Lightning Source LLC
Chambersburg PA
CBHW022202160726
48282CB00024B/289
* 9 7 8 8 1 1 9 6 5 4 0 9 3 *